USE
MELVIN
TO ACT
OUT.

From Pollen to

Stardust

How comfortable
we are
when the sun
leaves our grace..

Something
like children...

-Spaceman

Be Careful with your time

My dear Spacemen

Know your life is destined among the stars

The flowing essence of the Milky Way

The craters that made you strong

You are a galaxy.

Filled to the brim with endless possibilities

Starting Small
Laying unpaved
Baring no true foundation...
~~And like a small invader~~, not knowing your worth...
~~Seeing one~~; breeds the drinks of Kane.
Without courage
Legion will name itself ~~filth~~.
And litter both your mind and your lands...
Unnoticed
You will never see him switch your glass
Kill your son. Strip your fields ~~and women~~.
With~~out~~ your hands tied; tending the land ~~doesn~~'t seem like a burden.
For every seed planted
Your mind grows and children follow.
Do you not believe ~~eye's witness~~?

Then Check your lands before you rest your feet...
And Your Frame that has worked so hard to protect spirit.
Go
~~And~~ lie without notice.
Perhaps
birds may not know
They are blessed...

A Cloud's silver lining

The rainbow is nothing more than an illusion
The true pharaoh lies in the light
Flowing much like the thoughts of man into the ends of their ~~own~~ illusions
The fair, will tell stories of golden means
that have been given life through Midas.
He speaks...
"Word has spread
that without the achievement of the rainbow body;
Dreams of reaching the end of a rainbow have the same meaning as a butterfly
transforming into a caterpillar."
My people of gold lining and copper footing
Merchants have laid shop
Where you wash away your sins...
and as you spill the words "peace and love" like the venom of a snake
Know that as time passes;
your kin will have forgotten to carry a legacy.
And as the dog arrives home to rest his head...
Knowing that you will serve,
~~Only to beg when you need to feed his moments~~
However, you believe you are "master."
Does this remind you of something?
Or should I explain why the tortoise won the race

Be wary of hastily running.
Your mouth... Pride... Fear.... And all those ulterior motives that have stripped
~~your own~~ people of wealth
our

Look around
Reminding self to take lessons from the sloth
And see ~~your people~~ those, running...
Believing they are ahead in the race,

Hold On

Shaping nothing ~~into~~ *from* imagination...
the lost self, in its self
will try
but,
~~while looking for help~~....
Without photosynthesis,
The eye loses support

All of us are looking for the cosmos...
 in the things we hold and give ~~eye~~ glanced care...

What bares truth?
Is to love self and the flowing of rivers...
For we all come laced in the phoenix's knowledge.
We ~~also~~ forget infinity...
So we have to rediscover....
The moods and temperaments...
that ~~Forgetting~~ we were children....
Now nothing makes sense
Nor has the river forgotten that once
It was a droplet...
Teaching the child that sight is also beyond looking....
By passing gold through invisible veins
All of these factors are yours to know....
Become a flower blooming...

The Plea of a bee

A Hue that taught calm...
As I hovered and started.
carried and let go...
sharing in honey...
The wisdom to saturate the mind.
The honey-comb...
A place called home...
Hoping you notice before you take.
Your the pine-cone....

We both call home....

The Dying of the light

In possessing
One must obtain the thoughts of control and power...
In agreement to obtaining power

A bird is bound in station.
With only a section to stretch and to thrive
For the sky is no longer a lifestyle but a burden weighed and
snipped from tips...
The memory of soaring...
In being self....
When things were just things,
because life offers abundance...
Now Man offers water and the mundane...
Because they too are me
Bound in station
Wings snipped and freedom's thought.
A burden....
No difference the bird sings....
No difference

(Chirping)

After Victory

Welcome
drop your armor that flow the waves of crimson.
Leave the thoughts of lower self and lift your blade for those who fell into the
withering of things.
Hold fast to your handle.
For loose grip means death.
And faith without love
will lead you down the same road.

Listen Carefully
Copper knights of royalty and creation

Do not bath in the same pool that men have left their fifth and despair.
It is hard for men to understand what must be sacrificed for the soul.
Be cautious
of those who **do not sheath** their blade to the ignorance of
life

Their crown
only knows of the land of dirt and sorrow.
But;
if you wish to have the gold of Caesar.

Keep your armor and I
my tea...

The bloom

What is strange?
 is that I cannot hold water in hand...
for trying will leave me with longing and disappointment...
it will be here that life teaches me the lessons of flowing...
and as the wind swings into my life to whisper yesterday's
achievements....

Do not be in haste to question self!
Bring no snails to the race of horses.
for their blinders have taught nothing but tunnel vision....

Follow hope
And breath will crown your spirit in gold.
Become crude
And your shadow will not dispel when light gives rise.
Even so, clouds carry burdens...
Do not think yourself exempt!
And without the last of dragons
How will you conquer the fire in you?

Miss Universe:
                    Trapped in the faults of fallen angels

Find peace...
So clouds can bath your being
in sunlight and kiss the only place that matters.

Know the growth of the pine-cone...

Tribute

We are complex and scared...
So we carry strings looking for....
The sucka....

An electric socket...
 to bring rose complexion to cheeks.
A siren sings; a forgotten smile while she walks away.
As regret perches on shoulder
and recites tales of who you once were....

   So now you're carrying around strings looking for a sucka...
                                        I mean socket!

To gather a sense of self
For movements are without thoughts now
Also,
 You've forgotten
We are already connected.

When 300 fell

The heart known to all as the source of life will let you in on a secret...
One that will open a labyrinth to love...
Now,
You may lose your head to the sound of her voice
or be found burying your own heart in the sands of time...
competing for the title of Davy Jones...

The cost for this whirlwind
Is branded with the price of a rollercoaster ticket and will educate your
tones in all the ways of taking and receiving...

All the while man hunts in the earliest of days stalking a part of himself
that is gentle and unknowing that the world kills for sport...
A tone wails a question
Would you hear a tree fall if no one is around?
Would you love yourself if that word did not excuse sin with sacrifice?
Perhaps
Winter plays coach for your life.
Telling a season to be patient
while your essence bares all the warmth of the sun...
In time
A caterpillar cocoons
Much like you...

My Queen;
Who has been given everything but actual love?
Now, will show many
A butterfly's grandeur.....

So, here we are

As if finding peace is no longer a goal to keep.
Then let me bathe my tongue in blood...
Bring existence to the dragon now bound in ash and stories.

But you however...
Will not be remembered; for legion is one and unchained by
individualism.
Your worth
Is now of the essence of crimson glow and ohm's that carries no tone
Do you hear me?

My kin of shattered gold and the pearl of Ariel's teachings...
Uncrown yourself and learn.
Here is where suffering is sure.
Fear rampant and light unnoticed.

Here;
Is when you had the choice to see yourself removing your light in
previous agreements, thinking you will not be killed after the parlay.
In thought,
How is there honor among thieves?
For soul is what they collect.
Also, every king has spilled the words "survival of the fittest."
Do you not believe?
You've been an example of others crowning their selves?
Then pace your worth; before you choose.
To marry the red queen laced in silk and bone
Or commit to learning the beauty of Glenda....

In greeting self

Acknowledge the very existence of the sun...

Take notice in the sway of all trees,

The closeness of the blades of grass

The memory of water

In the pursuit of love

Find the daisy's hue to bring learning...

A sparrow's flight to be perspective

And mans survival to show conditions...

Calling forth chakra

The looming vulture in heavy tide
 waits for the moment,
when you are too weak to fight off survival...
                                        My siblings of stardust,
Fear carries the charge of the vulture and appears to know the
very secrets of Houdini.

Finding yourself in awe
Of how many friends really came to drink and forget their
worries.
"This having nothing to do with you"
But personal makes everything personal
and in return.
Flowers are picked,
birds caged
and love
encased in the lead of your chains...

The scrooge syndrome plagues the very streets of man.
However,
                    winter solstice
            is everyone's time for truth..

Good Shepherd

All the best love is given freely.
 to the ones who flock across golden meadows of hope
Praise worthy of kings
                    and those whose eye seems to shine brightest at dark….
 Allow no reign of king to outweigh your affairs…
Because now;
The very talk of love is tainted.
Placed in glass containers to be kept dry and without the experience of
life…
How can you save yourself without proper knowledge?

King of nothing but time wasted

Bare your arms in hate
Carrying a tongue that lashes the flesh from men…
You'll see;
The sweet grapes of conversation that change the topic from the
freedom of knowing
the golden gates which is your crown…
The devil looms
You should wait….

Let's give

We have all this
And to love; can be the ending of despair.
but the tongue
that is full of greed and loathing..
Will place relationships of all sorts into a corner;
paired with a dunce cap.
Trauma will ridicule and pose anything to be a threat.
those feelings
will chase a clock's hands and say it knows the world
after one rotation….
And with the wisdom of ignorance,
You can destroy and bargain free-will for the weight of a spool
of cooper.

Judas also played this very game
into a future.
We think is gold
carrying our own pains.
Looping again and again
obtaining everything but our sanity….

Chalice of Kane

The sliding grind of metal
Left driven deep into the crimson soul of flesh
The vulture looms into the afternoon waiting
Waiting...

Without crops
man cannot feed his family
Without love,
Carnage will introduce itself as a lost kin.

What will it take?

The shaping of golden metal to suit the sizes of ego...

When already crowned?

Hey Conqueror,

Of your own physical manifestations

When the men begin to rally and they will!

Will your spirit end with doves blessing our being with transcendence or will we meet with hounds bred by the tongues of men

And

the very venom of the serpent?

More than the lesser

The human experience grows to endless possibilities.
The lesser
will whisper your name under shadowy trees,
An a bed that terrifies the innocence of a child.
The lesser
is your ego that introduces you to pain,
and tells you of a wonderful friendship.
The lesser
will grant you wealth in the form of water,
and convince you to grasp tight...
The lesser
known by another name mental stagnation...

Now bound in a corner
There is more
Stories of heroes and their eye of truth...
The more
Is freedom from your own thoughts?
The chocolate that induces your happiness
The love you feel when you are loved as much as the sea....
The more
will not come looking for you.
The more
is what it is more!
And if you are not careful
The more
will make you greedy and filled with envy
The more
too much for the lesser
and not enough for itself.

Like egos part in the human experience......

Aye, Niggas

She will speak to you with poison on her lips
Look into you with lies and deceit.
But you'll still love her birthday suit....

She knows every word
to the perfect lie...
Asking if she can sing you a song that would steal your soul...

This will be your moment to shine
But you say
.
.
.
.
.
.
.
.
.
.
.

Yes!

Flowers and Dust

When Death agreed to come

Replying" They have to see me in a birds wings."

Mirroring self

But with an attachment

We branded him immortal to the reigns of king

And didn't notice him spawning children...

That look like us and play the life of men...

Now man kills man

and death no longer has to walk

For we all come to him....

Hey Sailor

Returning from the cold and barren

Did the rainbow greet you with the glance of Apollo?

Knowing the stars

Did they whisper why we fell?

Such time wasted...

Caught watching a rose bathed in an invisible vessel

Petals meeting barren stone

And again, we do not understand why earth rains.

Forgetting our own tears...

Pride does that

Calling the woes of alcohol

But what sailor doesn't drink and think of calypso?

The playing of an Orchestra

The Lioness

And these moments are but years spent following
Waiting in the brush with the purest of intentions
He speaks harmony towards hungry
But will not open his mouth to feed
Collect the flesh
Then wait...
Wait until?
The time to lunge all I have into the pride
Bathing in magnolia flowers
And the tricks of the possum

The Prey

Very well
Play the sheep until cloth falls from cloak
 and your intentions are shown
Nothing is more demeaning
than watching you conquer another consciousness.
Karma; will sing a tone
laced in white cloth and satin illusions
What is displeasing?
 is your nothingness
For I am sick to know you don't love life
Swimming in waters that bare no others
Empty
Dripping like quick sand...

Death

The raven sings a song
nothing but chatter
when insecurities come knocking
Showing the same truth when you uproot a tree
Run; In the place of the hare
Napping and tugging along with mindless play
Forgetting the joys of living
Allowing ego to take over
Don't think you can get far?
Such frets in life will be the length of their snake
Grabbing hold and not letting go
Slowly swallowing the tasteless imaginations and daisies painted the color of
marble
I'll come an remind you
I'll come!

No more!! the raven cries...
No more

Let us meet hubris

I've told love
To love is to!?

Then I waited
because in not knowing

assuming I knew,
That to love is to?

Again,
Silence
And like a child scared from the boogie man entering the room
Creeping close to implant fear
Softly brush a temple
All the while stealing a crown that wasn't adjusted....
Without confidence
It will present a kiss that freezes chambers and boards up the access to
think freely...
"I love you"...
I love you spills out fear's mouth
and I know...
That a flame burns
And temples were risen because of love
To love is to...
Love self

Come!!
Come!
Close your cage
and be silent
what better way for you to respect your master...
gave you the finest of pig skin
and wool to sheath your grief
Fed you
Your ancestors and queens on a Bronze tray
for a platter would make you grind your teeth...

The latest news is my hatred for your crowns
that have collected dust
like I have change.

Allow me to show you
Your gods now;
Drinks of lesser self
and toxins that will bathe you in exhaustion

Oh my dear boy...

My dear boy

Do not cry,
your mother never knew her worth
and the gift she has on man.

Matter fact here,
For you giving me your life
A Quarter
(laughter)
Of course you can have it in a bag to smoke
Now that I have more in my pocket

Psst..
for I no longer have to yell

Come
Come
Close your door
And sit quietly with my thoughts.....

Rocket

If strapping a rocket on her back wasn't enough
she threw faith in her pack.
she would sail
pass the remakes of pirates and lovers torn from the red queen's
ruthless words..
Truth is
"There's no going back."
She cried as the wind showed her tears harshness and freedom

Igniting her rocket ship
She'll pierce heaven
 while grey matter tails her spirit..

But will never catch up
She'll softly whisper "goodbye."
And if you listen carefully
Maybe you can hear her song of freedom

"She sailed on a rocket ship
With black lipstick
She didn't know where she was going
but she knew she had to save the world...."

This little piece of earth

In the roaring silence
her name is among the blooming of words,
reaching for the warmth of the tongue
and the passion after.
Appreciating the birth of her essence
Will grant you the temperature of the sun
when she smiles

However,
Bear in mind
she also brings a glance that strips away any cloaked
intentions
Her eye
Bares a truth that hibernates in you for the length of
seasons

The first step in obtaining this honey
Is listening....

Receipts

Nothing is more alluring then silence
To simmer you down
and listen to the instruments of life
A xylophone of breathing
The sweet hums of your heartbeat
The clashing tides of blood and essence
A symphony unlike anything heard and while the melody plays..
Truth is that
this comes from silence
A keeper of secret
Of unpleasant princes and uninvited guest
Of personal tragedy and the arising phoenix
Becoming a moment or an eternity
A sign of white flags or black flags
A place of strength or pride
A choice to wear a crown of light
or learn the malice placement of steel

The price of a rollercoaster ticket

In a single moment
Time shift
Removes itself from your space
and walks into another's life
        It may be here that a cricket shows itself to your thoughts
Helping you to know the growth of the spider
The removal of the snake's skin
the hardened shell from the crab..
                        maybe then;
        will you stand taller than yesterday

Our only fault is the belief in the mirror;
                        which tells us of the fountain of youth...
                        reminding us of who we once were.

            we would make different choices
        if the butterfly spoke of change to the caterpillar
        Who only looks upon them as an example?
                On that thought
            Who is your butterfly?
        If you need one to be in sight
            For a crown awaits you
            Once thinking begins

The birth of the drive-by

A communion meeting either in barren sands
or an orchard of honeysuckle readying for the bee to pollinate
This land
Much like a floating peninsula
can be found giving silence
Or the roaring cheer of the crowd.

Beyond these walls;
are Gladiators!
Birthed in copper tones and gold lining

And while their attire hang with stains of sweat and the gall of
the vulture

The inner coliseum contains a journey in which to travel
All the while learning
to lay shield down as the anchor to ones existence

Under the darken sky... She raged

Are we not tired from walking?
Bathing ourselves in a fog that takes away sight?
Why……. Are you eager to fill your lungs with grief?
Why ……Saturate the mind in yesterday's choices?
It is everywhere and it is nowhere
My Love
Are you not exhausted?
From turning around and slowing pace
The snake slithers into the mind
When self is spilled over with unrest
Allow your mind peace and calm
For you tug along tanks
thoughts that outer currency will guide you
That everything and nothing
My Brother
Sister
Keep running!

Hey survival

Grab hold of what you **learn**ed and place it into the soil of men
For life will water it daily
with the **language** of creation
To crown one self
is to dust off the leaves in your garden
Remembering that debris can be wiped away and forgotten
Apply this
to all the ways of men
Gardener of self
Are your thoughts consumed by perishables?
Then you cannot **teach** a gardener to tend their land
Are you upset by **truth**?
Then you cannot teach a boy to care for his flock
Do not be in haste to build a castle
Cementing your walls with anger
Will bring forth a dragon to your door
and your heart...

A party of crows

Wait for time to show you;
you
But to win the race
we rush
And the frame cast us out
To show the love of a frozen pineal gland

Can you hear it?
My love from Eden's garden

Do you know the sound of a hissing snake?
The marks left to the sand?
Still distracted by sinful things?

Show me the life of superman
and witness moments exposed to her emerald light
I've heard the cries
of "The damsel in distress.."
Also, seen her bathe in the ocean
And after,
threw a rock unto its waves..

Yes
Let her
Save her

Shhhh…

Allow me to apologize for knowing the sacred geometry of love and the burning
without

Who say this is yours'? A tree asks

Can I not hold my sister or

Are your roads more important than family?

Before we shared time and secrets

Now,

There is stillness in the breeze

I hope their existence is more than the plates that feed your kin

Or standing idly by waiting for you to return

Help me to understand

Who gave permission to make my home yours'?

Regardless,

before you I was here and after I will remain…

"What a lovely breeze"

Wolves on the street

Mind your manners
The vulture speaks
Driving their prey to the edge of sanity
All are here and there
and no where
In their own fabric of space
Stuck in moments
No man can gather but follow
"Bear witness" the judge speaks for sentencing
And then passes no law on kin
What last?
Is time
nothing more than a raven's travel,
A soul leaping, leaving nothing to the imagination
Most of us

Will remember Judas and his excuse for coin

All the while marching into the ivy
The past crying out old song for new change
And the coins tumble

lacing your cottage with no imagination games
But we speak of change
And the coins tumble

She tears his picture in half
then answers the call
To hear sorry
For no more sorrow
Plus a kiss on the neck
Having 3 more months before this is a situation again
But he wants change
The coins tumble

Bringing self to the end of its rope
Instead of standing
You turn away
When this is the moment to show life
a Childs smile..
And I want change

All the while
Money is being counted

A raised kite

Bound by release to know its own freedom
Will bind man in a lesson

"It was the manner on which the hummingbird's wings fluttered
That I understood nothing belongs to me.
That every stride has its own ripple"
Like light
And when in harmony becomes a silver lining
A bird's life among clouds
A mother seeing the birth of her child
Kissing slowly their forehead
Saturating her lips in what seems to be her own honey.

These moments can seem small
To closed eye's
Introducing nothing but the illusion of satisfaction
Similar to jack's mother tossing the beans
Similar to your gland that has learned
the still art of Medusa...

Tin Man

It's said

A bird chooses random pieces to nestle its nest

Maybe, one of those was your heart

But time frozen

between

a trampled watch and a splash in a river

Finds resting all the same

Blooming Lotus

Can you see the crown?
The shimmering draping of gold in pure form
Do not be upstaged by those who do not call you whole
Men who bare teeth only to lock tail in the shallow ends of body
Lords
Is what is known to us; Lords!
I say to men who do not know their worth
Share with me this fruit
Live
And know no nose of Pinocchio's talents
Sing no song of a sailor woe
Sure are golden rays and a quiet breeze
Like a dream
A dancer will place hands over eyes and touch heart
Love relates
and brings chocolate to soothe errors
Why?
Do you carry a lead box and shovel
Do you intend to play your own game of hide and seek?

Gingerbread stories

She spoke the words of the serpent
Looked heavily into my glow and told me to wait on her return
What peace do I have?
When no one can mimic the tale of the black mamba

She had the sweetest of nights
and whispered goodbye in the morning
While leaving me smiling
When the mirror gave press to steam
Her skin
The softest of lovers
Her crown
A child would never be scared of the dark
She was cosmic and the deepest tunnel of the volcano
essence poured from her being

Okay,
I may remember her slightly
Hoping you find home
Close by surround by trees
and the moon in perfect glow

"Be quiet!" said the forest

For she knows the life
of the first leaf in autumn

Simply Thought

This dangerous and eager mind wants to play with strings

Chaos knows its order

Following behind me into this fragile land;

to drink from the waters of wisdom

I know her smell all too well

She lingers in my thoughts

When all I have are shallow intentions

For life to think of me

Less than the stars

Where is my crown?

Two sides of a coin

The sun baths creation in love
Praises the ground with warmth and understanding
Feeds light to essence
Nurturing the suffering of darkness
This light
Has followed man from Eden
to the plains of Hades
With promise to create the wisest of men

Allowing seasons to pass
A man learns to love
But, not as much as a woman baring her soul

Roses of the red queen

It is believed in the lust of men
We find ourselves knocking on what seems to be our own limitations
                                    To know that if you continue forward
An oasis is only a loss of breathe
a fearful jump
a brood of jackals
and a unicorn saving away
            who said these moments have to bare physical form?

                        Once a crone asked her reflection
                        "Who is the fairest of them all?"
                And was anger when her imperfections answered
        It would had been better to ask herself that question in the dark
                                    naked with a lover

Hue you?
When thinking of wrath also give a moment for stillness
Obtain the image of a flower
Than step outside
The thoughts of confinement
The overwhelming sense of pride
That box that told you of cliffs and danger

Then step back inside
To bring peace
The swaying of all trees
The landing of a butterfly
And rage
missing from action
The effects of medusa only work
if you look in any idol direction
find your own perspective

a view line filled with length and clouds
a hand extended
time bowing for the patience you acquired
to merge with the ocean
learning the spirals ascent and descent
All;
to allow the growth of hue

The other side of the pillow

Morning came
With bright smiles
and flowers given in the form of a warm kiss
Between time and the locking of eyes
A rainbow bloomed between temples
Balancing peace
Found just when needed
These moments
When the inner child
Chases you around roots that flourish with the tree

A golden sky arrives
to bring warmth
And show the embrace of lovers

and like a snowflake landing on a crown
another kiss
shared between those who would die for their kingdoms
truth being said
"Peace rock shouldn't be the only time for a truce"

If you are ignorant

I will hope that you live in the shallow end of the pool and not be
tempted to float in the depths

For sharks do not know compassion for their prey
And darkness knows to fear the strength in men's heart
It is here

That you'll find life in knowing self

Yang to Yin

                                        I never expected sadness to come into my life
                                                                        but there it is
                                                        As sure as the hinges on a door
                                        Patiently waiting for a head nod and a warm smile
                                                                               Entering
Would feel like an ex-lover
A realization of past trauma
but a friend all the same
Holding close memories
when darkness played the songs of romance
                                                             Once again reminding
                                                            What it feels like to hear
                                                               a hollow "I love you"
But why not love again?
To fill a space that holds old pictures
and love letters
                                  Oh sorry!
There's my nod
And the seed to plant love again

In half the time

It must be easier to cover the face in what seems to be beauty
Plastered with pretty intentions and the best of hope
Giving care with application
The lover kisses your lips
 fills your cup with honey
Then helps powder your mind
With illusion
Knowing beauty only as a form

Later
she will apply an attitude
A Failed lover's sins
A time when she was innocent
Carrying love home
Faith clasp tight in both hands and forever
An idea without limitation
To be that memory again
So now
Application is a reminder of youthful freedom
An idea striving
a mothers' understanding
An elders tone
To only apply the basic foundation
Of what is the beauty of being woman?
Voices of ancestors
yelling give freely

Love!
Like fruit giving its best
To be pickled in a ready September

So your application
No!
Applying becomes
Truth

Applying a little pressure

Assuming that the rainbow meets man
With the intention of allowing the hand of Midas
Would it be proper for men to return with greed on his mind?

"Let everyone know of the dangers!"
Clouds warn
Learn or play the same cycles again
Tailing along with treats and a plastic bag
It is us;
that have become slaves to the average
It is us;
that have to learn through wisdom and acceptance

Become a tree
When change comes your way
Because in the camouflage
truth tells man
"To close with just knowledge
And I will cast your material wealth to piles!"
Heaven is within your rainbow and if you do not wear your light
A phoenix' life will follow you

To much!

Capturer of everything but self

Who will be responsible?
When you learn no one awaits you
but you

In the horizon watching
will always be greed and gluttony
Ready to introduce themselves proper

Silence interrupts
"Are you not me?"
Heaven, us?
Come home
And tell me of all your mistakes
That now have become lessons....

Too much softness

It will be hard to fold away like paper
Bury self between the lines of fiction and ill fated literature
All is willing
to become selfish
With our own version of love
Taking from its cup
and pouring its essence to the dead
But life
Drinks from the waters and carries nothing upstream
Our heads being in the clouds
Not noticing our feet in hell
Dragging self into the ruins of darkness
And lie dormant...

It would be hard for the soul to fold itself into paper
Truth is
It will carry you
Over mountains and streams
Only to find out
you could walk
That kind of selfishness
Nothing could have prepared me

Nothing but life

Watering the garden

The moon seems much brighter when on top a mountain
A fountain of dreams
 a safe to store memories
those stars seem close enough to catch
and let go
after filling with a wish..
                              Those moments
Now to know the comets distance
The slow rotation of karma

                              When releasing a dove
                              Tie your worries to the end
                              Or tie it to your wrist!
                              Like the adventure of a balloon
                              Or the idol time of a dandelion
                              waiting for the changing of mask

Pride seems much bigger when you are alone
Teaching the ways of the jaguar
The meteorite lost to impact
The darkened emotions caused by selfish reactions
Birds sing when they mourn
Screams release to expel the same

                              And love
                              being found after it all

Gladiator

Living life as man

I knew I may be bound for hell

So the rest of my time is spent learning self love

Finding happiness a sense away

The silent man speaks

It took courage the first time the words
came with a feeling
I would say
Similar to the spark in the eyes of love freed

Think?
Every time you fall in love
is that not the quality of you
or will you carry the ashes of a burnt out relationship
It takes courage
To help wash each other's hands
Mine being rough and bruised
However,
Knowing you are not fragile
A flower still comes to mind
Learning a different kind of strength is needed with woman
Some of us
not being able to see pass our shields
Us!
being warriors and soldiers
Forget to learn
It takes courage to admit
we allowed ego the reigns of king
Us!
making a jester out of love
And our people into peasants
Can I be forgiven?
If not by god than by your glance
An embrace that will help me to accept
A beast dwells in all of us
And also a snowflake

The Morning news

Thinking of the self
Feed your roots
Use nutrition as photosynthesis
And be cautious of hollowed marrow
Caressed by negative energy

The passing of this fruit
Fills the lips with the sweetest anti-venom
And he will lie
Pharaohs' who sacrificed their own race
for the building of ego..

Will now drown
in change and new beginning

Strange clouds that floated low

We shared an inner flame
Blazing fire
We danced to salvage the suffering
To escape the past
This blazing fire
From an unlatched birdcage
Formed diamonds from pressure
Jewels and pearls fell from the tongue
As love is freed
Then came
those orange rays with cinnabar streaks
Created from reactions
Later,
will come as chain bearers
Me being the first to show up and rage war
Now,
The first to warn men
like Scrooge

A fire blazes
We should be happy
We should dance

I hope you found thinking here

For I was not written

 to make you feel better

This is a **challenge**

For your **awareness**

For your dreams

For your birth

 and your death

I have faith you will find home in your castle

Ekillous

Please

Write a poem/ note/ message

And pass this book on to the next person

Pay it forward